About The Cover:

The image of Hebrew alphabet 'seeds' emerging from a pomegranate symbolizes my own learning trajectory, a lifelong journey towards knowledge and mindfulness. It is drawn from an old Hasidic folktale that tells of an uneducated Jew who wished to pray to G-d but was unable to speak Hebrew; indeed, he could only recite the Hebrew alphabet. As he did so repeatedly in the synagogue, the mystified rabbi asked what he was doing. *"The Holy One, Blessed is He, knows what is in my heart,"* said the man, *"so I am giving him letters that He can make into words."* The pomegranate often appears in my work as a reminder that according to the *Midrash* (commentary) a pomegranate contains *613* seeds corresponding to the *613* categories of *mitzvot* (commandments) that all Jews are required to perform in the process of spiritual development. The doves perched among the pomegranate and blossoms are traditional symbols of sacrifice, but here they represent the sacrifices that we must all make to preserve peace.

Other Titles By Ilene Winn~Lederer:

Between Heaven & Earth: *An Illuminated Torah Commentary*
The Alchymical Zoodiac: *A Celestial Bestiary*
Stitchburgh
The Little Sheep Who Couldn't Sleep

An Illumination Of Blessings

Illustrations & Text © 2014 Ilene Winn•Lederer

ISBN13: 978-0-692-27175-9
1st Edition
10 9 8 7 6 5 4 3 2

All Rights Reserved.
No part of this book may be used or reproduced in any form whatsoever or by any electronic or mechanical means, including information storage and retrieval systems without prior written permission of the publisher except in the case of brief quotations embodied in reviews. Signed, limited edition prints from **An Illumination Of Blessings** are available upon request.

986 Lilac Street
Pittsburgh, Pennsylvania 15217
(412)421-8668
ilene@winnlederer.com
www.winnlederer.com

With Love To
הקב"ה
For The Blessings Of
Family, Friends & Teachers.

And In Honor Of:

Mr. Jeffrey H. Lederer

Dr. Neil & Linda Feld
& Their Children & Grandchildren

Dr. Steve & Mrs. Juliette Zweig

Together We Are Illuminated.
I.W.L

An Illumination of Blessings

Ilene Winn-Lederer

Imaginarius Editions
Pittsburgh

TABLE OF CONTENTS

Artist's Preface : Ilene Winn Lederer
Introduction : Marc Michael Epstein

LIFE
Modeh Ani ◆ Shema ◆ Birth Of A Child
Blessing For The Home ◆ Blessing Of The Trees ◆ Shehechiyanu

SUSTENANCE
Netilat Yadayim ~ Washing The Hands ◆ Kiddush ◆ Birkat Hamazon ~ Grace After Meals
Blessing For Fruits & Vegetables ◆ Blessings For Bread & Cakes ◆ Shehakol ~ Various Foods

JOURNEYS
T'Filah HaDerech ~ The Traveler's Prayer ◆ Gomel Prayer ◆ Blessing For A New Endeavor
Blessing For New Clothes ◆ Mikveh ~ Immersion ◆ MiShebeirach ~ Recovery From Illness

SIGHT
Blessing The Sun ◆ Blessing The New Moon ◆ Thunder & Lightning ◆ Blessing The Seas & Oceans
Blessing For Unusual Animals ◆ Blessing For Beautiful Trees & Birds ◆ Blessing For The Rainbow

WISDOM
Asher Yatzer ~ Wisdom Of The Body
Blessing For Torah Study ◆ Blessing For Kindness
Blessing Between Day & Night ◆ The Birkat Kohanim

PEACE
Mezuzah Blessing ◆ Kaddish
The Seventh Blessing
Blessing The Sabbath Candles
Havdalah Blessings
The Bedtime Shema
◆ Psalm 136 ◆

During the research phase of my previous book, *Between Heaven & Earth: An Illuminated Torah Commentary*, I had been exploring the history and design of *incunabula* (early printed books) when I came across an old miniature prayerbook called a *Me'ah Berakhot* or 'One Hundred Blessings'. This meticulously crafted leather-bound treasure was a handwritten illuminated book commissioned in *1740* in Moravia as gift for a young bride. The original resides in a private collection in New York but in *1994*, Facsimile Editions, Ltd. of London, UK created a high-quality limited edition of *550* facsimiles that quickly sold out. I managed to locate one of these in the Rare Book Collection of Penn State University at State College, PA in *2012* and traveled there to examine it closely. Afterwards, I became curious about the ancient custom of reciting one hundred blessings a day and learned that it originated with an incident documented in the second book of Samuel *(24:2)*. In the time of Israel's King David *(1010-1003 BCE)*, the king took an unauthorized census of his people without understanding that the people Israel clearly belongs to G-d and that a man was permitted to count only what belonged to him.

Though David soon regretted his impulsive action, G-d gave him three choices from which to atone for this transgression; seven years of famine, a three-month lead ahead of his enemies in an inevitable war or a devastating plague that would last for three days. The fair-minded David went for the third option knowing that his family would be included in this punishment. He also hoped that a plague of short duration, unlike the other two choices would not decimate his people. When the plague had run its course, killing one hundred people per day, the sages then determined that each Israelite should sincerely recite one hundred blessings daily in appreciation of being alive. Perhaps divine irony was at play here, provoking David's *'yetzer ha-ra'* or evil inclination to take that census in order to institute this practice of one hundred blessings? Of course, no one will ever know. Nevertheless, the custom has remained integral to Jewish practice ever since.

Although the one hundred blessings are readily available in contemporary editions and portable pocket reminders, I decided that making a version for my own use with illustrations incorporating handwritten Hebrew blessings and their English translations should become my next creative priority. Illustrating one hundred blessings would be a challenging though worthy endeavor for me as an artist committed to exploring Jewish themes and I was willing to invest whatever time it required. However, at the end of *2012*, I became aware of **Project Kickstarter,** an online crowdsourcing platform that would allow me to raise funds to publish my work in book form. While preparing my presentation for this venue, I realized that the finite time period suggested to raise these funds and deliver a finished product would not allow me to do justice to the full project. So, instead of one hundred blessings, I decided to interpret thirty-six, carefully selected to cover typical activities throughout a given day and arranged by category. To my pleasant surprise, my *Illumination Of Blessings* project achieved full funding within a month! So I set to work, determined to keep the roots of this book in tradition yet allowing its pages to become wings of transition. The poignant words of Rabbi Tzadok HaKohen of Lublin inspired and focused my efforts as I journeyed through each illumination: *"Whenever you think of Hashem (G-d), He is thinking of you."*

May this small volume help enhance your own appreciation of our world's prosaic and profound beauty with which we are all blessed.

Ilene Winn-Lederer
Pittsburgh, Pennsylvania
July 30, 2014

INTRODUCTION

"Say a *bracha!*"
I remember this phrase from my earliest youth. And I have repeated it myself often, prompting each of my own children, until the age when they themselves began to ask—as Ari, my youngest has done recently—"What's the *bracha* (blessing)?" before partaking of food, or—as happened just last week—seeing a rainbow in the sky in the grocery store parking lot.

In religiously observant homes, the consciousness of the need to say *brachos* (plural) is pervasive. I always explained it to our kids by analogy to one's relationship with the owner of a store: one doesn't simply go into a grocery store and take what one wants—that would be stealing. One pays for the item in acknowledgement of the chain of gratitude that extends from that store back to the cooks and bakers who made the food, the farmers and herders who provided the raw ingredients, the earth that sheltered the seeds, the sun and wind and rain that nurtured them, and the One, the Source of Blessing, who created everything. To take food from the grocery store without paying for it would be stealing. By the same token it be theft to take an apple from a tree, or to extract a potato chip from its bag, or to enjoy the ocean, or the blossoming trees in spring without acknowledging their source in the One.

When I taught my second son Gabi *brachos* and *benching* (Grace after Meals), he was too little for all the Hebrew, so we simply taught him to say, in the case of an omelette, *"Thank you, Abba, for making my omelette, thank you chickens for laying the eggs, thank you farmers for taking care of the chickens, thank you HaShem (G-d) for making everyone and everything."* For *benching*, he learned the simple, rhyming Aramaic formula, *"Brikh Rahmana, Alahana, Malka Di-Alma, Morah Di-Hai Pita." "Blessed be the Merciful One, God, Sovereign of the Universe, Master of this bread."* These two gestures were attempts to instill in this very young child a sense of gratitude and awareness for the great chain of being and mutual interdependence, culminating in God—a God who is both transcendent Sovereign of the Universe, but also imminent Master of this food.

The problem in observant households and communities is that familiarity with blessings, and the feeling of being commanded to say them can give rise to rote recitation, concerned only with fulfilling technicalities. The concern for the recitation of *brachos*, particularly the correct *brachos* adds to one's awareness of the broad spectrum of Creation and to the necessity of categorizing them correctly within that spectrum. But a *bracha* rattled off in haste before tucking into a delicious peach cobbler does not necessarily extend one's spiritual awareness beyond ritual consciousness into the realm of mindfulness.

I remember telling my daughter Shevi at a time in her life when she was indulging her temper on Gabi even while she was learning to scrupulously observe ritual commandments, "You can't kiss the *mezuzah* with one hand and hit your brother with the other," or frequently reminding my eldest son Misha, as he reeled off the blessing for washing the hands before a meal at the speed of a Gilbert and Sullivan patter-song, *"God is very old and She doesn't hear very well, so speak LOUD and go S L O W."*

In obeying the commandments to recite *brachos*, it is easy to forget that they—like all commandments—require *kavanah*, focused attention. We may illustrate this with an example: a Jew so uneducated that she is not even aware of the requirement to fulfill the *mitzvos* (commandments) is out for a walk on the evening of Passover. She stumbles upon a box of peculiar square crackers on the ground, opens it up and eats one. Technically, she has fulfilled the commandment of eating *matzo* (unleavened bread) on the eve of Passover, but Maimonides, for instance, would aver that she has not, because the meaning of eating *matzo* on that night is to raise our awareness of the fact that God took us out of Egypt, and in order to come to that awareness, we need to be *mindful*, and in order to be mindful we need to pay *attention*, and not simply do things by accident.

Reciting blessings without proper attention and mindfulness is problematic only for the ritually observant, a small portion of the Jewish population. The vast majority of Jews do not say them at all. Moreover, many are totally unaware that the tradition requires blessings to be recited not just for ritual acts such as candle-lighting or eating matzo but for most aspects of daily life from washing one's hands to eating meals to caring for one's bodily needs.

It is unremarkable that Ilene Winn-Lederer—consummate artist and draughtsperson that she is—has chosen to address the questions raised by the practice of *brachos* through the visual medium. So many of our *brachos,* after all, relate to sight (or more broadly to sensual perception.) But it is highly remarkable, unusual, fascinating and precious that the volume you hold in your hands manages to sound a shofar call to mindfulness and to re-invigorating the tradition for all Jews. Neither a refresher for the observant, nor a primer for the non-observant, these illustrations totally renew the idea of blessings for those who uphold the ritual aspects, the spiritual aspects, both, or neither. They manage to lovingly honor the past while situating themselves squarely in the present and sending forth shoots towards the future.

I've often thought that Ilene Winn-Lederer is precisely the kind of Jew I would like to be—aware, attuned, buzzing with connections—certainly halakhic, midrashic, philosophical or poetic, but also visual, a thinking Jew, a thinking artist, a thinking human being, whose astonishing creative skill as an illustrator is wedded seamlessly with her thoughtfulness, playfulness and incredible depth as a religious thinker. Her explications of her work are invaluable. I would give my eyeteeth to know, in the case of the medieval illustrations I study, why the anonymous artist inserted the elements she or he did into the composition. Ilene, not content to let the illustrations speak for themselves, (though they certainly can do so) helps them along with engaging and often profound commentary, serving as Rashi on her own visual scripture. All this will ensure that, unlike my anonymous medieval limners, who I merely suspect of erudition and scholarly acumen, Ilene Winn-Lederer's name will go down in history not only as an artist but as a *talmidah chahamah*— a wise student of text and tradition, in her own right. Her words and the sentiments they embody are as beautiful as the brilliant illuminations on which they comment.

Blessings bring people together within the Jewish orbit. Minimally, three adults are required to recite the formal invitation to Grace after Meals. But saying *"Amen,"* (an acronym for *Adonay Melekh Ne'eman*— "The LORD is a trustworthy Sovereign,") loudly and clearly after the blessing links together the one who blesses and the hearer, as my beloved *Zayde* (grandfather) always used to remind me. I was recently out for a bike ride when I glimpsed, from a distance, a Hasid (strange in Poughkeepsie, New York) emerging from a Porta-Potty adjacent to the trail. As he washed his hands from a plastic water bottle, he recited the *Asher Yatzar* ("The One Who Formed Human Beings,"), the blessing said upon having relieved oneself. Riding past him in shorts, a tank top and a baseball cap, looking as secular as possible, I responded to his *sotto voce bracha* with a loud ***"AMEN!."*** which left him looking both puzzled and pleased.

Blessings can also unite people within the larger world community. Once we were in Jerusalem's Old City, with six-year old Gabi, who was sitting on a stone plinth eating a piece of pizza. When he finished, he recited, *"Brikh Rahmana, Alahana, Malka Di-Alma, Morah Di-Hai Pita."* just as a black-robed gentleman wearing a large silver cross and a (Christian) Orthodox clerical hat was walking by. He stopped, doubled back and said, "Please say that again!" with an enthusiastic smile on his face. It turned out that he was the Maronite Syrian Bishop of Jerusalem, a speaker of neo-Aramaic and was simply delighted to hear a little boy with a big *yarmulkeh* speaking "his" language. A nice talk afterwards made us realize that our vastly different backgrounds had let us bond not only over a common language, but over a common goal: acknowledging the Creator through His Creation. May it be that Creator's will to unite us all in this common goal. And let us say, ***"AMEN!"***

Marc Michael Epstein
Poughkeepsie, New York
15 Av 5774/ 11 August 2014

MODEH ANI:
An Appreciation Of Miracles

When we think of miracles, the big, cinema-worthy Biblical ones such as Noah's postdiluvian rainbow, the parting of the Reed Sea in Exodus or the appearance of *manna* in the desert usually come to mind. Such phenomena mysteriously appeared to precipitate a great crisis or in the wake of one and were meant to induce our fear, obedience, humility and faith in G-d. But in the absence of such grand miracles since post-Biblical times and under the influence of our scientific understanding of nature's laws, those reactions are fading into our collective memory. And as we live our mundane day-to-day lives, we blink past the one ubiquitous miracle we cannot afford to take for granted; waking up each morning.

Recited daily after sunrise, the **Modeh Ani** provides an opportunity to express our gratitude for the return of our soul to our bodies. Rationally, it can be said that we haven't gone anywhere; that sleep is merely a restorative, physiological process, but that only begs the question: why were we given the ability to sleep in the first place?

Judaism holds sleep to be of great spiritual importance. The late Lubavitcher Rabbi succinctly commented on the process of soul (*neshama*) renewal as we sleep and its return to us when we wake: *"If we didn't sleep, there would be no tomorrow. Life would be a single, seamless today. Our every thought and deed would be an outgrowth of all our previous thoughts and deeds. There would be no new beginnings in our lives, for the very concept of a new beginning would be alien to us. Sleep means that we have the capacity to not only improve but also transcend ourselves. To open a new chapter in life that is neither predicted nor enabled by what we did and were up until now. Sleep is necessary to free ourselves of yesterday's constraints and build a new, recreated self."* And so the **Modeh Ani** is our little reminder that every new day is a gift; a clean slate on which to become more of who we wish to be.

THE SHEMA:
To The Oneness of The Source of Life

In essence, the *Shema* prayer is an elegant dialogue between G-d and Israel. It announces G-d's unity while affirming the mutual love and faith that define and guide monotheistic Judaism. For humanity's part, the *Shema* provides a way for us to rise above our animal or baser natures. Though it is not a blessing per se, no book of blessings could be complete without it.

Although three verses comprise the full *Shema*, my illustration reflects the original *Shema* that consisted of only one verse from Deuteronomy *(6:4)* because it is relevant to the concept of blessings. The verse recounts the approaching death of the patriarch Jacob (also named Israel after his encounter with the Angel). Jacob's twelve sons are gathered at his side and required to state their faith in the One G-d in order to receive their father's blessings. The *Shema* is at the heart of morning and evening daily prayer services and may be spoken standing or sitting, privately or within a *minyan*. This is a gathering of ten individuals whose qualifications are defined by each branch of Judaism. Traditionally, one closes or covers the eyes with the hand to promote great concentration while reciting the first verse clearly and with emphasis to demonstrate its importance. I have attempted to express these ideas metaphorically in my illustration for the *Shema*.

In the blessing itself, if you look closely at the Hebrew words, you will see that the letters *"Ayin"* and *"Daleth"* are drawn larger than the others. This is because together, they spell the Hebrew word for "witness" to underscore the testimonial truth of this prayer. The central image of a tree whose leaves suggest human hands is set against background skies that represent the transitions between night and day. The hands replace the tree's natural leaves to illustrate the idea that all Israel is a tree whose trunk is rooted in earth and it's people are the branches reaching towards the heavens. I've shown the tree in the process of ascending towards heaven to address our yearning for divine correspondence. Some of the leaf-hands reach towards the ground as though to comprehend and incorporate the prosaic import of the blessing's sacred words. The small woman and man flank a large *mezuzah* or amulet as they recite the words of the *Shema* that are contained within it. My *mezuzah* is an original design employing the pomegranate motif. It is surmounted by a *chamsa* or hand for an additional measure of protection and insight.

The large letter *aleph* suspended above the tree of hands is drawn from the writings of the 15th century Spanish Kabbalist Rabbi Moshe Cordovero. It bears the Tetragrammaton form of G-d's Name and is meant to graphically affirm His Oneness. Our spiritual potential is visible through the aperture in the tree's trunk for it is my personal belief that we are all made of the stuff of stars to which we aspire even as we exist in this earthly realm.

A BLESSING FOR A NEW LIFE:
From Generation To Generation

The arrival of a new baby universally inspires joyful celebrations for the parents and community with festivities unique to every ethnicity and religion. In addition to an array of rituals and special foods, these festivities are marked by prayers and blessings offered to The Source of Life for the divine protection, good health and honor of this child. Because the essence of these events is the wondrous fact of a new life; an entirely new world of hopes and dreams, in the form of a tiny human being, I wanted to illuminate this blessing for a new baby to emphasize this idea alone. This would mean limiting my choices of traditional Jewish iconography that normally characterize my work. Since this cultural iconography often contains wonderful folkloric themes such as fanciful astrological imagery to promote '*mazal tov*' or good luck, this was quite a challenge for me as an illustrator; I am accustomed to crafting my images with much narrative detail, a pattern established in my previous book, **Between Heaven & Earth: An Illuminated Torah Commentary** *(Pomegranate, 2009).*

Nevertheless, I determined that in addition to the sleeping newborn child and colorful daffodils (which signify rebirth and new beginnings), I would limit my choice of iconography to the *wimpel* (or *vimpel*). This is a banner-like length of cloth that is wrapped and tied to secure the Torah scroll. According to Philologos writing in the Jewish Daily Forward, *"it is a tradition that began in late medieval times in the Rhineland city of Mainz, where the rabbi was then the renowned Ya'akov Segal (1360–1427). One Sabbath, so the story goes, a circumcision was under way in Mainz's synagogue, when it was discovered that the mohel (an individual especially trained to perform this ritual) had forgotten to bring a diaper in which to wrap the newly circumcised child. Since carrying was forbidden to pious Jews on the Sabbath, there could be no question of sending anyone to fetch one — and so the rabbi ordered the child swaddled in an avnet (a girdle or sash like those worn by the High Priest during the ancient temple service) that was removed from a Torah scroll. Afterward, when asked if it could be laundered and used as an avnet again, he ruled that it could be, inasmuch as it had not been profaned but had merely gone from one sacred use to another. In memory of the event, the Jews of Mainz took to donating the swaddling cloths from their circumcisions for avnetim, which they called Wimpel (the German plural is the same as the singular)."* Instead of the customary decorative imagery applied to *wimpels* by families who donate them to the synagogue, mine simply displays two Hebrew prayers, one traditional and one modern. Independent of its ethnicity or religious identity, the birth of a child begins a new page in the story of humanity. With this child, we have a new window into the mind and heart of the One whose children we will always be and Who will always cherish us.

FROM HOUSE TO HOME:
A Blessing Of Transition

The *Birkat Ha-Bayit*, a traditional blessing for Jewish homes worldwide, is often found on decorative plaques or hand-shaped *hamsas* (amulets) near the entrance to drive away evil spirits (negative emotional projections) and protect the individuals residing there. These are common gifts to the owner of a new house.

In the initial research for my illustration, a quotation from the Book of Proverbs told me: *"A house is built by wisdom and is established by understanding; by knowledge are its rooms filled with all precious and beautiful things." (24:3)* This is a powerful idea, but do these qualities also define a 'home'? Perhaps, yet having visited the homes of friends and acquaintances around the world, the unique flavor and ambience of each taught me that the difference between a house and a home is subtle, yet tangible. Beyond its physical structure and interiors, a house that can be called a home glows with an aura of peace, laughter and love. These qualities color it in a way no skilled decorator can truly emulate. Several examples of our innate need for shelter from Noah's post-diluvian resettlement to the long quest for a Jewish homeland are found in the Torah. The most picturesque, in the Book of Exodus *(Shemot Parashat T'rumah 25:8-9)* is where G-d requests that Moses establish a specifically designed sanctuary for His Divine Presence in the earthly realm so that *"I may dwell among them* (you)*."* It would seem that even the Source of all Life needs a place to call 'home'*!*

The house in my illustration is an amalgam of residential architecture drawn from around Jerusalem since it is the spiritual home for so many of us. Flanking the doorway are pomegranate and *etrog* (citron) trees; metaphors of the beauty, good health, fertility and *mitzvot* or good deeds that one would wish for the residents of the house. The *etrog*, central to the holiday of **Sukkot**, symbolizes our connection to G-d through our hearts. The cypress trees and the doves are symbols of sacrifice, seen here because sacrifices must be made within a household to insure peace and stability. The fish-shaped *mezuzot* on the doorpost and near the text address blessing and abundance as drawn from the verse in Genesis *(Bereshit 48:16)*, *"And they shall multiply like fish in the midst of the earth."* The Hebrew letter *bet* is included in this illustration because its original form in the proto-Semitic languages of the Middle Bronze Age resembled a tent-like shelter or 'house'. It also begins the Torah with the word B'*reshit* (In the Beginning) and the word *'baruch'* for blessing. Philosophically, *bet* represents the dualities that define Creation (dark, light, good, evil, male, female, etc). The forms of fruit and their leaves inspired the design of this letter because in a sense, their trees were among the prototypes of shelter from weather and predators. The antique bronze key is included because it enables us to enter the idea that when a house becomes a home, it also becomes a metaphor of memory; a repository of touchstones that connect us to ourselves, to each other and to the larger world beyond our doors.

ברכת הבית

בזה השער לא יבוא צער
בזאת הדירה לא תבוא צרה
בזאת הדלת לא יבוא בהלה
בזו המחלקת
בזאת המחקה בזה המקום
תהי ברכה ושלום

Blessing For The Home

LET NO SADNESS COME THROUGH THIS GATE.
LET NO TROUBLE COME TO THIS DWELLING.
LET NO FEAR COME THROUGH THIS DOOR.
LET NO CONFLICT BE IN THIS PLACE.
LET THIS HOME BE FILLED WITH THE
BLESSING OF JOY & PEACE.

THE BLESSING OF TREES :
Poems Upon The Sky

Like the universal languages of music and art, trees speak to us without words, inspiring us to describe them with our own words and visual expressions. In Deuteronomy *(Devarim) 20:19-20*, we learn that even in wartime is life precious and that trees are essential to our continued existence: *"When thou shalt besiege a city a long time, in making war against it to take it, thou shalt not destroy its trees by forcing an axe against them: for thou mayst eat of them, and thou shalt not cut them down; for is the tree of the field a man, that it should be besieged by thee?..."* Equally eloquent are the words of the late Lebanese poet Kahlil Gibran in his collection of aphorisms, Sand And Foam: *"Trees are poems the Earth writes upon the sky..."*.

I am reminded of these ideas during the festival of *Tu B'Shevat* (the 15th of Shevat on the Jewish calendar), the minor Jewish holiday that celebrates the renewal of trees and the abundant gifts they provide for us. The Blessing Of The Trees *(Birkat Ha'Ilanot)* is a lovely way to express these sentiments. Although trees are spoken of in the blessing for certain fruits, I chose to work with a blessing for trees that also delight our sense of smell with their beautiful fragrance.

The tree shown here is an imaginary one that integrates both qualities, bearing several varieties of fragrant fruit and their corresponding flowers. Nesting at the apex of the tree is an ornate golden Torah crown and in place of its trunk is a *yad* (Torah pointer). Unlike the traditional single-handed instrument used for reading Torah, this one has two hands. Together, these images remind us of our stewardship of this planet and of the Source of Life Who has given us trees not only for our sustenance but as a model for the *'etz chaim'* or Torah staves that support our 'Book of Life' and as an eternal symbol of Earth's partnership with Heaven.

THE SHEHECHIYANU:
A Blessing For Here & Now

Throughout the Jewish year, a day or more of holiday observance or of a major festival distinguishes many of the twelve months. These are intended to celebrate and preserve our history and culture while bringing them forward to our present and future. Although the liturgy for these holidays addresses them individually within their duration, there is one blessing called the *Shehekhiyanu* that is traditionally recited during candle-lighting on the evening preceding each of the major holidays and festivals. Holidays that commemorate sad or tragic events such as *Tisha B'Av* (the destruction of the Temples) are the exception.

The *Shehekhiyanu* is a blessing of thanks acknowledging special occasions and life-cycle events such as weddings and bar mitzvot. It is also appropriate for new or unusual experiences; tasting a first fruit in season, meeting an old friend, or acquiring a new home or clothing. '*Shehekhiyanu*' is Hebrew for *"Who has given us life"* (and brought us to this moment). This blessing originated in the Mishnah and is cited in the Talmud, the collection of Jewish laws, interpretations and observances codified after the destruction of the Second Temple in Jerusalem in the year *70 CE* (of the Common Era).

My interpretation of the *Shehekhiyanu* blessing is relatively straightforward, showcasing symbols of the Jewish holiday cycle shown clockwise from the top: *Tu B'Shevat* (pomegranate tree), *Purim* (Megillat Esther & *grogger* or noisemaker), Passover *(Pesach)* (seder plate & Passover lamb), *Lag B'Omer* (sheaf of wheat & city of Jerusalem), *Shavuot* (tablets of the Ten Commandments), *Rosh Hashanah* (Torah crown, shofar & prayerbook), *Shabbat* (a Kiddush cup and lit candles represent this weekly celebration), *Sukkot* (Lulav & Etrog), *Shemini Atzeret* (rain & clouds), *Simchat Torah* (Torah scrolls with harvest symbolism) and *Chanukkah* (menorah & dreydl).

This 'cycle of life' is suspended between the sun and moon in reference to the Hebrew lunar-solar calendar that determines when each holiday begins and ends. In this system, the year corresponds with the solar calendar and its months match the lunar calendar. I've placed the moon at the upper right-hand corner to indicate that all holiday observances begin at sundown the previous evening.

Though the *Shehekhiyanu* blessing is not part of our daily observance, awareness of it can help us savor every moment of all that life offers us.

NETILAT YADAYIM:
The Waters Of Life

The mundane act of washing our hands assumes a wholly different quality when it is done within the context of blessing. By reciting the **Netilat Yadayim** after performing its prescribed ritual, we raise the concept of cleanliness to holiness and align ourselves with the Source of Life through this *mitzvah* (commandment).

Creating an illustration for this blessing seemed simple in the beginning, but after drawing numerous studies of hands and water, I had the unsettling feeling that something more was at play here. If the act of washing one's hands was intended to be a holy one, how could I interpret it as such? The answer was found in the early portion of Genesis *(B'reishit)* that recounted the separation of the upper and lower waters during creation. Connecting these events to the fundamental idea that we are conduits for holiness in this world led me to build images that compelled the inclusion of the alchemical symbol for water, one of the four elements at the foundation of existence.

In my illustration, two icons for that element are suspended between the upper and lower watery borders that frame it. The frame also supports two *'mems'*, Hebrew letters that begin and end the word *'mayim'* for water while their shape represents its waves. This is to emphasize the importance of water not just as a medium for cleanliness, but as a metaphor of the wisdom of Torah which quenches our thirst for knowledge of the esoteric and the mundane aspects of our daily lives.

THE BLESSING OF WINE:
A Taste Of Sanctity

The Torah in all its fullness of parable and instructions for living suffers from no lack of attributed metaphor or simile. It has been compared to a 'tree of life', to a mirror designed to reflect life from *its* unique perspective, and to water that satisfies our thirst for knowledge and wisdom, among others. The Torah's complexity has also been likened to wine; both reveal their own secrets when digested just as they provoke us to reveal ours when under their influence.

For these reasons, wine has always been blessed as the ubiquitous 'guest' at every Sabbath and Havdalah observance, at holidays and festivals and at Jewish lifecycle events. In its own way, it is a messenger of the dualities of Creation for it is able to summon joy from sadness, yet allow sadness and solemnity when these are required.

Although the figures in my illustration for the **Kiddush** or blessing over wine are dressed in the garb of medieval vintners for visual continuity in this book, they are meant to recall the tale in the Book of Numbers of the twelve scouts led by Joshua and Caleb that were sent ahead of the Israelite camp to appraise the nature of the Promised Land *(BaMidbar /Parashah Shelakh-Lekha 15:38-40)*. Their exaggerated accounts of what they had seen included an enormous bunch of grapes, fit for consumption by the giants who purportedly lived there. The image of Caleb and Joshua bearing this botanical phenomenon inspired the couple balanced on the large pewter *Kiddush cup* that is perpetually filled by their sanctified grapes so that its bounty may flow to the four corners of the earth.

בָּרוּךְ אַתָּה יְיָ אֱלֹהֵינוּ מֶלֶךְ הָעוֹלָם בּוֹרֵא פְּרִי הַגָּפֶן

Blessed Are You, Source of All Life and Sustenance, Who Creates the Fruit of the Vine.

THE BIRKAT HAMAZON:
Food, Glorious Food!

Apart from those who regularly recite the blessings after each meal, I suspect that more expressions of gratitude for our food go to our servers in restaurants or to the chef for a meal well-prepared and thoughtfully presented rather than to the more ethereal Source of Life. Though I have not always done so, in recent years I've decided to try and experience my meals as more than just substances to satisfy my appetite. When I choose to appreciate the combination of colors and textures, the unique fragrance of each item on the plate or acknowledge the complex processes that made this meal possible, it becomes a gift of nourishment for my body and soul. These thoughts and the memories of fine meals past led me to the image that illuminates the **Birkat Ha-Mazon** or the Blessings After Meals.

The origin of this set of blessings can be found in *Devarim* or Deuteronomy *8:10*: *"When you have eaten and are satisfied, you shall bless the LORD your God for the good land which He gave you".* These consist of four distinct but related ideas expressed in a lovely poetic stanzas. They are: the *Birkat Hazan* (blessing for nourishment and praise for the One Who Sustains the World), the *Birkat Ha'aretz* (blessing for the Land of Israel), the *Binyan Yerushalayim* (blessing for the rebuilding of Jerusalem), and the *HaTov V'Hameytiv* (blessing for the One Who Is Good and the Who Does Good). Following these blessings, a group of short prayers beginning with the word *HaRachaman* (The Merciful One) ask the Source of Life for compassion.

Although several versions of the **Birkat Ha-Mazon** can be found within Judaism (Ashkenazic, Sephardic and Yemenite), I've chosen the Ashkenazic form with which I am most familiar. Accordingly, the illustration includes medieval Jews of Central and Eastern European ethnicity, my own cultural background. On the table, the pewter dinner service is empty indicating the conclusion of a meal. Since the figures portrayed are not nobility, their durable pewter might have been more commonly used than finer metals or porcelain.

Suspended over the group are four items reflecting the concepts of the blessing's four verses listed above; a winged crown, a jar of biblical manna, a lion and a model of Jerusalem surmounted by a living date palm. Each item has its mundane and mystical purpose. At the conclusion of particularly satisfying meal, we may rarely ask ourselves whether we live to eat or whether we eat to live. But if this question occurs and if we choose the latter sentiment, then maybe a little mindfulness will help us realize how to make everything we eat that much tastier… and to achieve, as the French Ashkenazim might say, 'Be' te-avon' (Bon Appetit)*!*

EDEN'S EDIBLE BLESSINGS:
Fruits of The Tree & Earth

Although we are told in the book of Genesis *(Bereshit,1:29)* that *"God said* (to Adam), *"Behold, I have given you every seed-bearing plant on the face of the earth, and every tree that has seed-bearing fruit. It shall be to you for food,"* no specific varieties of fruits or vegetables are named. This was especially true for those on the Trees of Life and Knowledge where the fruit of the former was said to maintain health and immortality while the fruit of the latter was off-limits for human consumption as it granted the self-awareness that led to human mortality. But just as insatiable human curiosity provoked the expulsion from Paradise and determined the fate of humanity, so did it lead to discoveries over the ensuing centuries of the nutritive and medicinal properties of earth's produce for our bodies. It is probably safe to venture that the fruits and vegetables we eat today are not wildly different from those in the Garden of Eden with the exception of our cleverly cultivated hybrids; the results of our scientific manipulation of those original species.

So what does all this have to do blessings? Nothing--if you are a strict evidence-based rationalist, believing that all life on earth evolved of its own unscripted volition and that we are so intelligent that we've figured out how to use it to our advantage. But if, by acknowledging the divine source of our bounty and the intelligence behind its beautifully intricate design and purpose, then reciting a blessing for these creations is surely in order, since foods exercise our senses of sight, smell and taste as they provide our souls with healthy shelters. My childhood existence as a creature of instinct and need evolved in time towards the realization of all the ways from which we can choose to enhance and maintain ourselves. How hard is it to stop and think before taking that first bite of apple or tomato and murmur a little thanks to our Source for our partnership that makes it all possible? It's not; it just takes practice.

Traditionally, for a tree-borne fruit to receive the *'Ha-Etz'* (tree) blessing, it must come from a perennial tree that doesn't renew its stem or grow too close to the ground, such as apples, figs, dates and plums. Fruits of the earth that receive the *'Ha-Adamah'* blessing include all vegetables, legumes, peanuts and any fruit that is not covered by the **Ha-Etz** blessing such as melons, bananas, pineapples and strawberries. For this illustration, I've paired the blessings for fruits of both tree and earth and selected several varieties to represent each. These were chosen for their visual harmony and worked into a design to form a border around the blessings. All the produce is set against a black background of 'earth' from which all originates and is renewed.

THE HA-MOTZI BLESSING:
A Toast To Bread

Bread, in any of its forms goes far beyond satisfying our hunger. If we pay attention, it lets us taste the histories of civilization in every bite as it nourishes our bodies and spirits. In the Books of Exodus *(16:1-36)* and Numbers *(11:1-9)*, bread first appeared as a mysterious substance called *manna*, 'given' to the early Israelites *only* during their desert tenure. It was ground and baked into cakes that purportedly tasted like honey or any other food one wished to imagine. Though *manna's* true nature remains a mystery, it has been associated with coriander seed, 'kosher' locusts', hallucinogenic mushrooms and bdellium, a sort of resin, perhaps from the tamarisk tree. Upon reaching the Promised Land, the *manna* disappeared and the Israelites learned to cultivate grains, turning them into 'real' bread for both home and ritual use. For the latter, only breads baked from wheat, barley, spelt, oats, or rye were permitted.

The *'ha-motzi'* blessing atop my illustration is for any bread made from the aforementioned five grains. Its inital letter is embellished with loaves of pita, the Sabbath bread of biblical times. The blessing below is the *'mezonos'* recited over baked goods like cakes, pastries, cereals, cooked rice and grain goods like pasta or couscous. The stalk of rice among the five species of grain in the borders of my illustration is included for its esthetic beauty and for its use in the Spanish (Sephardic) Jewish tradition that adheres to Orthodox customs with differences in interpretation.

The breadmaking process from harvesting to oven to table is embodied in two figures: a woman carrying a sheaf of wheat and a baker standing behind a sack of flour and a pantry scoop. The stone quern beside the woman was for milling grain. The type of round challah under the baker's arm is often used on the *Rosh Hashanah* holiday and signifies the wish for a long life. The baker is also holding an oven paddle or 'peel', a tool that has been in use since ancient times to move loaves of bread and baked goods in and out of hot ovens.

If you look closely at the challah in the center of the illustration, you will see a tiny number 78 baked into it. This detail was suggested by *gematria*, a Kabbalistic system in which the numerical equivalence of the letters and words of Torah is calculated for interpretive purposes. Accordingly, the word for bread *(lechem)* is valued at 78, a number derived by adding together its letters *lamed (30)*, *chet (8)* and *mem (40)*. That G-d's Name is equivalent with the number 26 and appears in the *Birkat Hamazon* or Grace After Meals recited three times daily is no coincidence. Three times $26 = 78$ a number that brings us full circle as we acknowledge our Creator and the miracles of life.

THE SHEHAKOL BLESSING:
Eating With Ethos

From the moment G-d 'breathed' the soul of life into Adam's nostrils, we were made to understand how our noses and souls are gateways to experiencing our existence. Shortly thereafter, Adam and Eve were instructed concerning the source of their nourishment: *"Of every tree of the garden you may freely eat. But of the Tree of Knowledge of good and evil you shall not eat of it, for on the day that you eat thereof, you shall surely die" (Genesis 2:16-17).* Overcome by curiosity, they disobeyed, giving birth to the history of religion. Ironically, scholars and rabbis reasoned, the first couple were not punished merely for eating forbidden fruit, but for the way in which they ate it; without the intention of holiness, without gratitude for its Source. But how do we define gratitude?

A simple 'thank you' may suffice for most occasions, but does no justice to our deeply felt emotions when we are on the receiving end of a kind word, service or unexpected material gift. That is where blessings allow us to be more creative in expressing those emotions, not just to our fellow humans, but to the One whom we credit as the true Source of such gifts.

When it comes to food, a blessing does more than address what we are about to physically consume. Though we eat to strengthen our bodies and healthfully house our souls, each time we do so, we also recognize our senses of sight, taste and smell that connect our physical and spiritual essences. Judaism offers many specific opportunities to spiritually acknowledge the wondrous elements of life on this planet. But for those times when we wish to recognize a food that doesn't fit clearly into an established category, there is the *Shehakol* or 'everything' blessing for those singular forms of nourishment. It is recited before eating or drinking any foods other than 'fruits' of the earth or trees, wine, or breads. The types of foods included under the *Shehakol* rubric are: meat, chicken, fish, cheese, mushrooms, wild herbs, some edible flowers, eggs and soy-based products. Drinks include: water, fruit juice, fruit smoothies, tea, cocoa and coffee. This blessing also covers some 'manufactured' foods or those prepared with combined ingredients such as soups, candy, ice cream, peanut butter or baked desserts like apple pie. However, the ingredients used for these combined foods should not be recognizable within the product in their original form to qualify for the *Shehakol*. If so, they would require individual blessings such as the ones recited for fruit of the trees or the earth. Detailed information on this blessing and its rules may be found online, in contemporary publications and in classic texts such as the *Mishnah Brurah* and the *Shulchan Aruch*. The mere existence of the *Shehakol* blessing in our complex legacy rarely fails to amaze me. However did the rabbis and scholars formulate a blessing to appreciate and acknowledge foods that never existed in their time?

THE TRAVELER'S PRAYER:
For The Journeys Ahead…

Historically, travel has always been fraught with anticipation, excitement and potential hazards. *"Have a good (or safe) trip"* and *"Be Careful!"* are phrases often directed at us or by us to friends and loved ones setting off on journeys large and small through the various stages of our lives. While every culture has its own distinctive way of conveying these sentiments, embellishing them with a prayer to the One greater than us seems to make them 'official', almost as though offering a 'magical' protective amulet to the traveler. Indeed, in the Jewish tradition, small cards printed with these prayers are readily available in bookstores and online. When you are gifted with one of these, it somehow lends gravitas to your journey. Most travelers' cards contain only the prayer in Hebrew and English with little more than a cursory border to contain them. So when I decided to illuminate the Traveler's Prayer or ***T'filah Ha-Derech*** for this book, I was determined to visually enhance it with images pertaining to the words of the prayer.

Accordingly, I've set the words into an antique map border to suggest a history of travel and navigation that is both timeless and time-based. The alchemical elements of earth, air, fire and water within the border are both the basis of our earthly existence and the forces that drive the various means of transportation that we've developed over the centuries. Between them are an astrolabe that might have guided us to our destination by the sun or moon and stars, a pair of sandals that might have carried us along rivers or over mountains and deserts long ago and a tiny tent, symbolic of the way stations on our journeys with their own potential risks for the traveler. Though we are conversant with methods of travel through the ages of iron, steam and air, we are only beginning to understand that we may soon travel beyond our own planet. That heady anticipation accounts for the lesser-known fifth element shown here; the aether. In classical mythology, 'aether' personified the 'upper skies' of space and heaven. I like to think of it as the worlds of our imagination, where we may travel unhindered by earthly concerns. Nevertheless, one might wish to use caution when traversing our inner landscapes. While the insights and ideas we discover there are often exciting and rewarding, they, like our dreams, may not always be what they seem…

BIRKAT HA-GOMEL:
A Blessing For Well-Being

The *Birkat Ha-Gomel*, a blessing of thanks for well-being is one that I did not have the presence of mind to recite when, a few years ago, I was involved in an automobile accident that nearly totaled my car. Fortunately, I was not seriously injured, escaping with minor bruises and the aftershocks of a mental earthquake. But at that time I should have intoned the *Birkat Ha-Gomel* in appreciation for having experienced and recovered from a life-threatening situation.

Although life-threatening situations can occur in varying circumstances, the *Birkat Ha-Gomel*, which originated in the Talmud *(Berakhot 54b)* was drawn from *Tehilla* (Psalm) 107 which describes four prescribed situations that merit recitation of this blessing. Symbols for these are shown with *sefirot* (divine energies) that represent their spiritual counterparts: *1.* **Upon completion of a sea voyage** *(The letter Chet on the ship at sea tells us that the sea refers to Chochma, for the vast expanse of Divine wisdom)* 2. **Upon crossing a desert wilderness** *(The letter Ayin represents the barrenness of a spiritual desert where our minds and hearts are not in accord)* **3. Upon recovery from illness or childbirth** *(The letter Bet refers to Bina for understanding during a trying time)* **4. Upon release from captivity** *(The letter Dalet represents the value of Da'at which connects the emotions and the intellect, a connection that may be blocked by captivity)*. The Torah breastplate that anchors the acanthus leaf border points towards the *tzedakah* (charity) container in which a monetary contribution to the community may accompany the recitation of the *Gomel*.

When the Temple stood in Jerusalem, anyone who experienced these situations would be required to bring a live sacrifice *(korban)* of thanksgiving, but the *Birkat Ha-Gomel* is now an acceptable alternative. According to Rabbi J.H. Hertz, former chief rabbi of the British Empire, it may be recited after any extraordinary escape from danger. In the Orthodox tradition, this blessing is also recited publicly among a *minyan* or quorum of ten men, although Conservative and Reform traditions include women in this number so that an entire congregation may acknowledge an individual's survival and recovery from one of the above situations.

Whether I visually interpret a Torah *parashah*, a passage from Talmud, a folktale or as in this case, a blessing, I like to explore such texts on multiple levels so that you are not seeing merely a literal illustration, but rather one that invites you to draw your own interpretations or ask more questions. While I hope you will never find yourself in any precarious situation that requires its recitation, it might not be a bad idea to keep a copy of the *Gomel* blessing at hand…

THE MINDFULNESS OF A NEW ENDEAVOR

On the eve of *Pesach* (Passover) *2014*, my illustration for blessing a new endeavor was completed. Although I don't believe in coincidence, this was a fine instance of synchronicity because this holiday is the epitome of a new beginning; an epic physical and spiritual journey in the history of the Jewish people. Each new endeavor that we undertake, regardless of magnitude is a microcosm of it and can be seen as a journey of sorts, independent of whether we leave our homes, workplaces or travel outside of our comfort zones to accomplish something new to our experiences. When we are creating a work of literature, art, music or science, I believe that we are doing so in a partnership with a larger intelligence that requires it of us. This 'larger' intelligence may be a numinous, spiritual entity or the multifaceted imaginings of the collective 'threads' in the human tapestry. Either way, our endeavors make us each a significant thread in that tapestry: an entity alive with potential.

In this illustration, the artist and artisan Bezalel is imagining the works he will design for the *Mishkan* or Tabernacle in the desert. Per the instructions received at Mt. Sinai through Moses, he must build a structure and ritual implements to mirror their heavenly counterparts. As he gathers the letters of an animated early Hebrew alphabet, Bezalel is enacting a symbolic tribute to his relationship with the Creator and demonstrating their mystical role in the creation of the world and in the artisan's terrestrial model of it.

One of the ritual objects will be the Ark of the Covenant destined for the sacred enclosure within the Tabernacle. Only the High Priest is permitted to enter this 'Holy of Holies' on *Yom Kippur* or the Day of Atonement. The Ark's cover will support the two *keruvim* (cherubim) to protect the Tablets of the Law. Its chest will also contain Aaron's blossoming staff with a jar of *manna*. Bezalel's drawings for the Ark are on the papyrus scroll in the foreground along with the Egyptian-influenced ink palettes and drafting tools that he might have used. Some of these are in the pocket of the artisan's work apron as well. Behind him, on the vertical loom is a tapestry woven with likenesses of the keruvim. It will become the *parochet* or veil guarding the Ark that is meant to provide a virtual glimpse of its guardians to the congregation of worshippers.

At sunset, when Passover Seders begin worldwide, we are compelled to consider the holiness of this observance, celebrating even its mundane aspects. Yet their meaning would be diminished if we did not consider that every endeavor we undertake contributes to life's larger experience for each of us. By understanding that what we create for our own needs and pleasure can enlighten and benefit others, we acknowledge and thank the One Who created us for the realities we continually create together.

A BLESSING FOR DRESSING:
Garments For Our Souls

Just as our skin conceals our interior systems, its visible condition is designed to describe their functional state. Likewise, our clothes in their myriad styles and colors both conceal and reveal our psychological states even when our thoughts, speech and actions might proclaim otherwise. But in a perfect world, the clothes we choose to wear would project not merely the public image we present, but would serve as 'soul garments' to reflect our inner character via the dynamic facets of our souls. This blessing is found in the *Shacharit* (morning) service and was designed to clarify our understanding of why and how we clothe ourselves. It is traditionally recited over a new article of clothing when worn for the first time.

A verse in *B'reshit* (Genesis *3:20*) that relates how our primeval ancestors wore only their 'birthday suits' during their time in the Garden of Eden initiated my work on this illustration. Upon their expulsion from that ideal environment, the first couple were given a 'garment of skins' for protection from the mercurial elements beyond it. These garments were not described until many centuries later. According to a *midrash* (rabbinic commentary on the Torah) called **Pirkei D'Rabbi Eliezer**, the serpent that provoked Adam and Eve's illicit behavior did not go unpunished. Because Sammael (the serpent), could not die, he was condemned to boogie on his belly and made to shed his skin every seven years. This 'skin' was then made into the garments for the first couple.

No serpent appears here, but you might imagine a shadow of him in the sinuous length of linen framing this illustration. My 'first couple' are dressed in medieval European style garments and shoes derived from both plants and animals. Their shoes are of leather and their clothing made from the plant fibers (of either flax, hemp, cotton or wool). Note that the sheep and cotton bough are depicted below the flax and hemp plants to illustrate a *'chok'* known as *'Shaatnez'*. This commandment prohibits combining wool and linen in a piece of clothing and is one of four *'chukkim'* in the Torah (inscrutable, compulsory commandments). The woman holds a large fig leaf to recall Eve's initial response to her newly mortal predicament. Their clothing also reflects the tenets of *tznius* (modesty) in appearance. This custom of dressing encourages seeing past one's clothes to his or her inner attributes.

The symbolic construct of the Ten *Sefirot* (Divine Energies) held by the man is the Hebrew letter *'vav'* which corresponds to G-d's name and hosts the other nine letters. Rabbi Yitzhak Ginsburgh of the Gal Einai Institute explains that while clothing protects us against the elements, it also signals our soul's character traits and enables connection to our Creator. Finally, mindfulness about how our clothing reflects who and what we are, may one day inspire us to understand and perhaps re-experience the perfect world in which we were conceived.

MIKVEH:
A Journey To ReBirth

Although I had listened to tales of *mikveh* experiences from my mother and others, the idea of ritual immersion meant little to me until my first visit to Israel with my husband in *1974*. On our tour of the 1st century CE fortress of Masada, we explored the once-luxurious remains of King Herod's palace that included a *mikveh*, or ritual bath. Peering into its now dry depths, I imagined being in the footsteps of my ancient ancestors and hearing echoes of their struggles for spiritual cleansing, closeness with G-d and a measure of sanity in those stress-laden times. This grand complex was later taken over as the desert outpost by a community of Jewish zealots in their rebellion against the Roman rule of Jerusalem. The Masada tour motivated my curiosity to learn more about how the ritual was carried out and why. However, the opportunity for in-depth research into this subject did not assert itself until *2013* when I began work on this book and decided that it would include the *mikveh* blessing.

Even though my personal background to date did not include the religious or social impetus to visit a mikveh, I learned that the ritual of *tevillah* (immersion) is one of three essential *mitzvot* or commandments reserved for women. Mikveh, which literally means a collection of water in Hebrew, is more than a pool of water. According to Tractate Mikva'ot in the Mishnah (the 2nd century CE codification of the Oral Torah), it must be a bath designed with specific dimensions and capacity to hold water that is stationary but which originates from a flowing natural source (a lake, ocean or rainwater) to permit ritual and spiritual purification.

Today, despite the long and often painful history of Judaism, immersion in a mikveh remains a viable practice among observant Jewish men and women. Many modern *mikvaot*, while adhering to those classic dimensions, also exhibit an awareness of the necessity for religious and spiritual continuity. These have been designed to resemble stylish, well-appointed spas such as the Mayyim Hayyim *mikveh* in Newton, MA. The setting of my illustration, an early *20th* century mikveh in Israel whose water can be seen flowing into it from the passageway beneath the stairs, was inspired by a beautifully made *1997* film called **"Women"** directed by Michal Bat Adam and Moshe Mizrahi. Here I have shown a young woman with two attendants who are required to observe her immersion and ensure that it is done properly. Three stars, seen through the tiny window in the background signal the onset of the Sabbath, a traditional time for this ritual. Usually a sign displaying the immersion blessings is posted near the pool but with a bit of artistic license, I incorporated the words into the water itself suggesting that like water, our history has been mercurial, yet the consequences and benefits of using it mindfully are eternal.

MI SHEBEIRACH:
A Blessing For Body & Spirit

The *Mi Shebeirach* is a blessing that may be recited individually or within a minyan for those in need of healing, whether spiritual, physical or both. The name comes from the opening verse of the prayer, *"May the One Who Blesses"*. Its words were set to music by the late singer Debbie Friedman and has become her best known work.

The first recorded appearance of this blessing was in the 12th century French prayerbook, ***The Vitry Mahzor*** compiled by the Talmudist Simcha ben Samuel of Vitry. It's original intention was to petition for the well-being of the community and indeed its essence is preserved in the *Amidah*, as one of the set of prayers recited three times daily. But in recent times, in both Reform and Conservative practices it is recited after the Torah reading and includes the names of specific individuals (usually their Hebrew names) in need of healing by those praying on their behalf.

The centerpiece of my illustration for the *Mi Shebeirach* is a majestic *Aron Ha Kodesh* (Torah ark). Its open ornately carved doors reveal small bird-like slips of paper floating towards a vision of Jerusalem that represents the Torah. According to a 300-year-old practice, these *tzetlach* (notes inscribed with prayers) are placed in the crevices of the Western Wall at the site of the ancient Temple where, the Talmud teaches, all prayers ascend to Heaven. A gravely ill woman who is the subject of the *tzetlach* lies before the Ark in hope of recovery. Historically, cultural response to illness has been both colorful and naïve. To reflect this, the illustration includes a healing amulet upon which a Caladrius bird is perched. In medieval bestiaries, this mythical bird would determine the fate of an ailing person by the position it assumed relative to the patient. If it faced the patient, recovery was assured.

As I thought about the significance of the *Mi Shebeirach*, I realized its core message: that we must partner with G-d Who is The Source of Life by participating in our own recovery or in that of a loved one(s) to the best of our ability, whether it be through seeking medical intervention or by recognition of an ailing spirit that can manifest as physical illness. Forgiveness of oneself and others is one of the elements at the core of this process. Although the future outcome of serious illness is often unclear and sometimes all we can ask for is strength to endure, I feel this blessing speaks for all of us living and working together as community to understand the bigger picture of life and our role in it.

מִי שֶׁבֵּרַךְ אֲבוֹתֵינוּ וְאִמּוֹתֵינוּ אַבְרָהָם יִצְחָק וְיַעֲקֹב, שָׂרָה רִבְקָה רָחֵל וְלֵאָה, הוּא יְבָרֵךְ אֶת הַחוֹלִים וְיִרְפָּאֵם. בָּרוּךְ הוּא יִמָּלֵא רַחֲמִים עֲלֵיהֶם לְהַחֲלִימָם וּלְרַפֹּאתָם וּלְהַחֲזִיקָם וּלְהַחֲיוֹתָם. וְיִשְׁלַח לָהֶם מְהֵרָה רְפוּאָה שְׁלֵמָה מִן הַשָּׁמַיִם, רְפוּאַת הַנֶּפֶשׁ וּרְפוּאַת הַגּוּף, הַשְׁתָּא בַּעֲגָלָא וּבִזְמַן קָרִיב. אָמֵן.

MAY THE SOURCE OF ALL LIFE WHO BLESSED OUR ANCESTORS ABRAHAM, ISSAC & JACOB, SARAH REBECCA, RACHEL & LEAH, BLESS & HEAL THOSE WHO ARE ILL. MAY THE BLESSED HOLY ONE BE FILLED WITH COMPASSION FOR THEIR HEALTH TO BE RESTORED & THEIR STRENGTH TO BE REVIVED. MAY G-D SWIFTLY SEND THEM A COMPLETE RENEWAL OF BODY & SPIRIT & LET US SAY, AMEN.

BIRKAT HA-CHAMAH:
A Blessing For The Sun

On average, we spare little daily thought for the sun other than to its perceived influence on the esthetics of the next twenty-four hours. It is, therefore, we are. But on the fourth day of Creation when the sun first appeared in the skies, it began an endless story punctuated only by the myths and folklore of every human culture since the beginning of recorded time. That story is an amalgam of theological speculation and scientific discovery seasoned with a pinch of millennial fear mongering for spice; a small part of the collective effort to comprehend our origins amidst our mercurial environment, the relentless cycle of the seasons and our place in the cosmos.

Of all the blessings in our cultural canon, the **Birkat Ha-Chamah** or Blessing of the Sun is the most rare because it is recited only once every twenty-eight years, most recently in April of *2009*. It is not to be found in standard prayer books; its text is distributed to participants at each recitation ceremony. The blessing dates back to Talmudic times *(1st century AD)* when the rabbis, wishing to acknowledge the sun's importance to life on Earth without inviting idolatry, addressed the star theologically without attributing divinity to it. According to the Babylonian Talmud, the **Birkat Ha-Chamah** is to be recited every twenty-eight years on the vernal equinox in order to commemorate the sun's return to its original position (relative to the Earth) on the fourth day of Creation (when it is fully visible above the horizon at dawn). The rabbis taught: *"One who sees the sun at the beginning of its cycle...recites: 'Blessed is the One Who made the Creation'." (Tractate Berachot 59b)*.

My illustration for this blessing is set in medieval Europe when rabbi-scholars like Maimonides (the Rambam) and Samuel ben Judah ibn Tibbon engaged in lively discussions of Torah and Talmud, codifying their opinions for future generations. On a grassy hillside against the backdrop of a castle fortress-town, a man and his son wearing their prayer shawls are awaiting the full sunrise as they imagine a vignette of the fourth day of Creation framed within an astrolabe. The five-fingered hand-shaped *(hamsa)* device from which the astrolabe is suspended represents the idea that we are to use our five senses to praise G-d. The *hamsa* is also referred to as the Hand of Miriam in recalling her role as sister to Moses and Aaron. The boy holds a ram's horn *(shofar)*, which will be sounded when the sun has risen. This image was suggested by the **Birkat Ha-Chamah** ceremony of *April 8, 1981*, led by Rabbi Zalman Schachter-Shalomi who stood on the observation deck of the Empire State Building in New York and sounded the *shofar* amidst a crowd of *300* participants.

Perhaps through this rare blessing we can understand our place in the cosmos as witnesses to the wonders of created life; we may question it, but never learn the answers at the end of the story; at least, not yet...

BIRKAT HA-LEVANA:
A Blessing For The New Moon

Our moon had always been an ancient source of wonder until July 16th of 1969. On that day, American astronauts walked on her and became at once part of her history and future in human perception. Although they showed that the moon was physically no more than a large, cratered and lifeless asteroid, unworthy of the age-old mysteries attributed to it, they changed little for most of us earthbound creatures in terms of our romantic, spiritual or prophetic predilections. Yet, whether we are romantic or pragmatic, we can safely admire her subtle beauty. She lights our paths at night and reminds us that we are not alone or without purpose in the dark: ideas that likely gave rise to the many moon-centered religious rituals over the centuries, even in Judaism.

In Rabbinic tradition, the freshly minted Israelites were commanded to sanctify the new moon upon their delivery from Egypt. *"This month shall mark for you the beginning of the months; it shall be the first of the months of the year for you." (Shemot/Exodus 12:1-2)* While that practice directly conflicted with Egypt's officially sanctioned sun worship, it also ensured that the moon would not become an object of worship. Instead, its cycles became the basis of the Jewish calendar, a valuable tool for timekeeping and agricultural foresight in which each month is defined by one lunar cycle of the moon around the earth. The *Rosh Hodesh* holiday that marks the beginning of a new month is a hallmark of this system. It is observed with prayers and blessings when the moon's orbit suspends it directly between earth and the sun, its thin crescent visible to all. Passing through its phases, the moon illustrates our 'deliverance' from spiritual darkness to light. It is interesting to note that the monthly cycles of both women and the moon figured in the establishment of Rosh Hodesh as a holiday because both are capable of rebirth or renewal and must be honored as such.

Another related monthly prayer is called **Kiddush Levanah** or The Sanctification of the Moon in which we express our appreciation for G-d's celestial gifts. It is traditionally performed outdoors in the moonlight (preferably under a cloudless sky) at the end of the Sabbath from 3-7 days after the new moon is visible. In the Talmud *(Sanhedrin 42a)* Rabbi Yochanan teaches that one who blesses the new moon in its proper time is regarded as one who greets the *Shechinah* or the feminine aspect of G-d.

In my illustration for The Blessing of the Moon, both observances are addressed. The sun has just set beyond the distant mountains. On a hillside above the sea, a woman wears a *tallit*, or prayer shawl and dances to the rhythm of her tambourine as she raises a cup of water in tribute to Moses' sister Miriam and all Israelite women who crossed the *'Yam Suf'* or Reed Sea after the Exodus from Egypt. Four phases of the moon from new to full, from darkness to light are aligned along the ethereal form of a nocturnal quadrant, an instrument used in medieval times for astronomical navigation, perhaps for a ship like the caravel arriving with the tide. These represent the human curiosity and ingenuity at the conflicted cores of both science and religion while the woman on the hill instinctively knows that only love, peace and gratitude will mitigate their discord if we understand the dualities in the gifts we have been given.

Blessing For The Moon

Blessed are You, Source Of Life, Who Makes the Heavens By Your Word & the Heavenly Bodies By Your Spirit. By Your Laws Of Time & Space Do They Reveal Their Set Purpose. You Order the Moon To Renew Itself As A Shining Crown Over Your Creation. Blessed Are You Who Renews The Months.

A BLESSING FOR ELEMENTAL MAJESTY

We can't mistake or ignore them. Like the rain, sun, winds, and snow, thunder and lightning remind us of our place in the moment, celestial bookmarks, if you will. They assault our senses and extort our reluctant humility regardless of how clever and powerful we believe we are. Ancient cultures, their divinities and religious rites were by-products of the awe and terror their dramatic appearance commanded. When the growing sophistication of monotheism began to dominate much of human society, its scholars and poets attributed a more subtle intent to them.

In Judaism, a custom developed to recite two separate blessings for thunder and lightning to recognize their different qualities. Both are represented in my illustration. Though he did not know the origin of this custom, the 16th century Polish Rabbi David Ha-Levi Segal in his commentary on the **Shulchan Aruch** speculated that perhaps the roar of thunder signals its dominance over lightning and suggested that the blessing for lightning can be recited when either are seen, especially when seen together. Ironically, the **Mishnah Berurah** (227:5) and the Talmud (*Berachot 59a*) both consider thunder more potent than lightning even though it cannot be seen. Indeed, the Talmud states: *"Thunder was created only in order to straighten the crookedness of the heart,"* lyrically reminding us to ask who created thunder and lightning and why? From a religious standpoint, the answer is indisputable.

My first visual response to this blessing was to show only a dark sky with bursts of lightning, leaving the noise of thunder to the imagination. But as I traced the history of our developing comprehension of thunder and lightning, I suddenly wondered, were there any recurring shapes or patterns in a storm's bursts of lightning? Could they form some sort of heavenly message? Ok, ok, I know this whimsy is magical thinking. But then, I'm not a meteorologist with hard knowledge of the electrical and mathematical characteristics that might explain its technical structure. So I let my imagination travel back to the revelation of the Law at Mt. Sinai. Could the thunder have been meant to call our attention to lightning's shapes and patterns inspiring ancient minds to create the letterforms of an early paleo-Hebrew language? I soon envisioned a rare single cell thunderstorm hovering over the mountain, wondering whether its winds, shaking the burning bush on the mountain, also whispered meaning into Moses' ear? As the illustration progressed, I couldn't resist allowing a tiny lightning bug onto it, illuminating the wonder and complexity of our existence.

Presenting the blessing in this fanciful light makes me wonder whether this divine 'skywriting', if it could be correctly transliterated and translated might be key to comprehending our destiny in the *Sefer Chaim* (Book of Life)?

SAILING THE SOUL OF CREATION

Although orbiting satellites send us spectacular images of the swirling seas beneath a clouded Earth, these views pale next to our physical comprehension of their vastness and power from our perspective of dry land or from the decks of our ships. As we marvel at the unknown depths from where some pre-conscious form of us emerged, the magnitude of the sea speaks to the essence of what we are. The sea, if you will, is the soul of Creation.

Observing that the Earth's waters dance on its tectonic armature in time to the moon's allure and the mercurial winds has provoked the fear and wonder inspiring the religions and myths of many cultures whose livelihoods depend on the seas. Prayers for the safety of their fishermen, travelers and for the lands on which they live are central to these systems. Where these prayers were once directed at individual deities deemed to control our planet's natural forces, Judaism offers the **Birkat Ha-Yam,** a special two-part blessing for the seas and oceans. One part acknowledges Creation as it addresses the large-scale wonders of nature while the other is directed at a specific large body of water that must have existed since the six days of Creation and must not be land-locked.

No one has ever agreed upon which ocean fits this description, but rabbinic opinions in the ***Shulchan Aruch (228:1)*** point to the Mediterranean Sea for this blessing: it was probably the largest one in their own experience. Unlike those prayers for divine mercy and protection from the elements, the verses of the ***Birkat Ha-Yam*** acknowledge our wonder and humility at the constancy of Creation.

The images for this blessing were influenced by our ancient and complex relationship with our aquatic ecosystem. While an ordinary seascape might have sufficed, the ***Birkat Ha-Yam*** begged for a more nuanced visual narrative. What then came to mind was an illustration I'd created for *Parashat Eikev* in *Devarim* (Book of Numbers) for my previous book, ***Between Heaven & Earth: An Illuminated Torah Commentary.*** It showed a grandfather and granddaughter metaphorically listening through a conch shell to the still, small voices in their hearts.

My collection of oddities includes such a shell, found on an Atlantic beach. I like to imagine the sound of the seas echoing from its inner spirals and so the shell, open to reveal the 'heart of the sea' became the centerpiece of this blessing. Within the conch is a tiny 15th century Spanish caravel that may be sailing on a trade mission for its merchant owner. With a nod to the Biblical Leviathan, a watchful piscine creature swims lazily anticipating the coming time of Messiah.

Below, the conch's compatriots nestle among a watery scape of seaweeds. In the morning sky above, a faint moon observes the four winds competing to guide the ship to its destination as the seagulls survey their boundless territory. At last, even when I thought the illustration was nearly done, I still couldn't resist playing with one last image. Can you see the tiny hippokampus hiding among the sea wrack?

BEASTLY BLESSINGS:
For Extraordinary Creatures

The elaborate weavings of words and inventive images that grace medieval illuminated manuscripts have always been a source of fascination for me, particularly as I considered how to interpret this blessing. It appeals to me because while it acknowledges and praises our Creator for the rare and extraordinary animals that inhabit our world, it differs from the similar blessing for beautiful creatures in that it recognizes those that are not conventionally attractive.

Selecting one or two from among such myriad creatures appeared to be a difficult choice until I found some helpful references in the Talmud *(Meiri, Berakhot 58b)*, the Code of Jewish Law or **Shulchan Aruch** *(225:8)* and the *Gemara* (rabbinic teachings compiled after 70 C.E.) which opined that the blessing should be recited upon seeing a monkey or an elephant. Monkeys and elephants have physical qualities that resemble those of humans such as the monkey's body shape and manual dexterity and the elephant's smooth, hairless skin and trunk that it uses like a hand.

While monkeys and elephants are common sights today at any zoo, they were considered exotic and rare in medieval times, inspiring the creation of special blessings. In my early research, I found that elephants were often depicted saddled with *'howdahs'* that sometimes resembled castle towers. Further reading revealed that the word *'howdah'* is from the Hindi and Arabic languages referring to portable shelters used for travel but also for hunting and military battles. Carvings of elephants wearing *howdahs* are often seen as pieces in chess, the symbolic game of war.

The concept of my illustration for this blessing was finally clarified by a discussion of the elephant as a metaphor of the Torah presented by Marc Michael Epstein in his classic book, **Dreams of Subversion in Medieval Jewish Art and Literature** *(Penn State University, 1997)*.

Taking this idea a few steps further, I imagined that a *howdah* could also represent a sort of portable synagogue; an ideological 'castle' as its own metaphor of Jewish history. Accordingly, the small monkey representing our animal souls is riding high on an elephant who represents our divine natures and whose *'howdah'* or 'turret' recalls a medieval synagogue. This structure was inspired by an illustration in a 15th century volume of the **Mishneh Torah** written by Moses Maimonides in the 12th century. A decorative border of fanciful flowers and dragons surrounds them in tribute to the master medieval illuminators whose timeless work continues to inspire my own.

BEHOLDING BEAUTY:
A Blessing Of Appreciation

"*Beauty is in the eye of the beholder,*" goes the old cliché, but this is a quick sound bite at best because it doesn't attempt to define beauty nor offer insight into any alternative, more subtle perspectives on it.

At first glance, the blessing recited upon seeing something beautiful in our world seems similar to the one recited on encountering a fragrant tree. Both are found in the Talmud *(Tractate Berakhot, 58b)* and both express appreciation to our Creator for the gifts of Creation and for our five senses as they serve to enhance perception of our environment. The latter focuses on the sight and smell of certain trees while the former also recognizes trees and includes the esthetic beauty of humans, birds and animals that we acknowledge with our senses of sound, touch and taste. The words of the blessing seem simple enough, however the concept of beauty in life is anything but. So choosing elements to represent this blessing's intent was quite a challenge. I knew that I needed to portray some sort of tree along with a person, animal or bird, however, I decided not to include a person for this blessing. I did not wish to single out one specific ethnicity as an archetype for a human being.

Consulting my sources for the other elements in this illustration, I found a commentary by Rabbi Abba of Acre, a third century Palestinian commentator on the Oral Torah that offered the *etrog (citrus medica)* as a likely candidate for the Garden of Eden's Tree of Life, though no one really knows what fruit it might have borne. This information remains a mystery to prevent extinction of its species in the biosphere because of its association with the expulsion from Eden. He suggests that in addition to the pleasant flavor of the fruit, Eve found the wood of the *etrog* tree edible *(Genesis 3:6)*. A later authority, Rabbi Abahu, the second century commentator from Caesaria, translates the word *etrog* as *'ha-dar'* or fruit that dwells in both its young and old phases, on the tree through all seasons. The *'pri etz hadar'* or fruit of the beautiful tree is described in the book of Leviticus *(23:40)* and has been cultivated in ancient Judea for more than 2000 years. The fruit is said to symbolize the human heart for it represents a person who is able to internalize scholarship and also perform *mitzvot* or good deeds. At this point, the *etrog* tree became my obvious choice for this illustration. I've given it 22 *etrogim*, symbolizing the 22 letters of the Hebrew alphabet that according to Kabbalah, are the building blocks of Creation.

For my choice of beautiful birds, the commentaries offered the fine examples of peacocks and parrots since these species are unique for their graceful forms and beautiful colors. The cockatoo, once known as the crested parrot, was added for compositional balance. To complete my illustration, the blessings in English and Hebrew are embellished with initial caps constructed from macaw parrot and peacock feathers respectively.

Perhaps this blessing will inspire your appreciation of the beauty around us and its Source, if and when we remember to truly open our eyes.

THE RAINBOW:
A Covenant Of Blessings

When the shadow of a rainstorm has passed and we are able to witness a rainbow illuminating our corner of the world, we are often reminded of the patriarch Noah's post-diluvian rainbow; a sign of divine forgiveness for human global corruption and the promise that another cataclysmic flood would never again decimate nearly all life on this planet.

Inspiring this illustration was my recollection of a wonderful tertiary rainbow that appeared over the east end of Pittsburgh in the late *1990s*. Its three overlapping arches stretched from Squirrel Hill to perhaps somewhere beyond the North Hills. Regrettably, that was before the convenience of iPhone cameras that could easily record it. Nevertheless, I still remember that it appeared in a sky of an unusual grey-green color that made it seem so much brighter. Suspended in the majesty of that moment, I didn't care that science views the colors of the rainbow as wavelengths of light traveling at particular frequencies or that their visibility depends on our vantage point relative to the sun's position and the presence of sufficient raindrops to refract and reflect its light. From my perspective, that rainbow just seemed too magical for such mundane explanations.

Among the mystical interpretations of natural phenomena, I found an interpretation of the prophet Ezekiel's colorful vision of the *Merkabah* (Divine Chariot). It was an intriguing admonition to remain humble in the presence of holiness. Further readings alluded to the presence of **Shekhinah** (the feminine aspect of the Divine) and to the *sefirot* (numinous energies underlying our reality and the spiritual state of our souls) whose colors correspond to the rainbow. Fanciful folktales drawn from commentaries on the Book of Genesis were both cautionary and poetic in their concepts of divine justice, mercy and repentance in the face of transgression. These ideas suggested that the Torah itself is like a 'rainbow' whose colors reflect our spiritual character as we respond to its message.

Soon, my mind's eye flashed on the image of the **Shekhinah** wearing a *tallit*. This prayer shawl is often compared to celestial wings and the **Shekhinah** to a holy bird that protects Israel during the centuries of exile. I liked this idea for its reference to the sacred feminine. Its stripes, though traditionally black in color can also lend themselves to rainbow symbolism as demonstrated by Rabbi Zalman Schachter-Shalomi's tallit. In designing it, his intention was to wear a physical meme as a reminder of Creation in the light of G -d's unity. Eventually, these concepts and my memory of that tertiary rainbow took shape in my imagination and led to the imagery that accompanies this blessing. My **Shekhinah** wears her rainbow *tallit* beneath her crown of feathers (to mirror the bird metaphor). She also balances a crystal that reveals the four elements (air, earth, fire and water) necessary for our continued existence. Her cloven-hoofed 'feet' are a fanciful interpretation that is also drawn from Ezekiel's vision.

If what we imagine gives us comfort, fosters doubt or amuses us, we can also learn how important it is to keep wondering and embellishing these ideas for generations to come.

ASHER YATZAR:
Blessing The Wisdom Of Our Bodies

The need to relieve ourselves is such a constant part of our lives that we generally give it little thought except when we have difficulty doing so. Even when the difficulty passes, we simply get on with our days. Our habit of taking these processes for granted is exactly why it is important to be aware of a blessing called the *Asher Yatzar* (*"Who has formed* {humankind}*..."*).

Rabbi Schneur Zalman of Liadi, the founder of Hasidic Judaism, calls man *"a world in miniature,"* with its own inner seas, skies, forests, animal correspondences and rhythms all working together as they propel us through the 'galaxy' of our real and virtual worlds. In a sense, our bodies are barometers of the earth and this blessing expresses our thanks for letting these natural processes flow as they should so that we may stand in humility and respect before our Source of Life.

The *Asher Yatzar* blessing, composed by the 4th century Babylonian Rabbi Abaye became part of Jewish tradition when it was compiled by the *Sanhedrin* (Sages of the Great Assembly, *300-500 BCE*). Many details concerning the behaviors surrounding it can be found in Chapter 3 of the *Shulchan Aruch* (Code of Jewish Law). Although the rabbis of that time did not understand scientifically how our bodies functioned, they knew instinctively that if one or more of its components became blocked or impaired, it would be impossible to remain alive. Common wisdom maintains that reciting this blessing conscientiously will aid in promoting good health and longevity.

My illumination for this blessing centers around a fanciful likeness of Rabbi Abaye whose internal construct of the *sefirot* (divine energies) correspond to each of his external limbs and internal organs. These are embedded within elemental icons that characterize each bodily function. His shadow image follows as a reminder that each time we relieve ourselves, it is a though we are reborn with a new appreciation of how beautifully we are made.

Blessed are You, Source of All Life, who fashions our bodies with wisdom. Should any of our intricate systems malfunction, we could not stand up before You. We offer praise & thanks to You for our health & strength.

THE WISDOM OF TORAH:
Blessings Hidden & Revealed

At first glance, the blessing traditionally recited prior to reading the Torah appears to be merely a formal expression of respect for this foundational document of Judaism. But it's much more. It is a way we can express our gratitude to the Source of Life for the opportunity of partaking in this sweet and savory feast for our minds, bodies and souls.

With this blessing, we honor the moment when Moses descended Mt Sinai with the divine gift of our 'spiritual DNA' : a gift of timeless and inestimable value. I like to think about this gift in the metaphoric terms of information science, where data is transmitted to its destination via virtual electronic 'packets'. Similarly, the Torah can be seen as a compilation of concise 'packets' of instructions for how to live and steward our planet embedded with the assurance that the Source of Life would bless us always; if and when we accepted them.

Extending this idea, we can think of each encounter with Torah as akin to meeting a person for the first time. Although we recognize that Hebrew is the language of Torah and that a person's physical features define them as human, how do we account for our immediate physical and/or emotional reactions to them? It may be that information and impressions are transmitted between individuals in virtual packets via a delivery method we do not yet understand or control. Only thought and time spent with that individual allow us to 'unfold' these 'packets' to understand our initial reactions and determine the character of that relationship.

In the same way, the Torah reveals her meanings to us gradually through time and thoughtful study as we learn to see between her lines. Perhaps the oddly-named scholar and convert to Judaism, Ben BagBag, quoted in ***Pirke Avot*** (Ethics of the Fathers) said it best: *"Turn the Torah over and over for everything is in it. Look into it, grow old and worn over it, and never move away from it, for you will find no better portion than it."*

The Torah is masterwork of infinite, unfathomable depth: a virtual blueprint of Creation that I have attempted to encode visually in this illumination. Though we cannot fully decode its mysteries, it will always be there to keep our curiosity and questions alive and to help us maintain our dialogue with the Source of Life.

THE BLESSING OF KINDNESS

In our visual media-oriented world, we often encounter posters, bumper stickers or heartwarming newspaper columns that urge us to **'Perform Random Acts Of Kindness'**. Isn't it strange and sad that we should need to be reminded? But given the complex duality of human nature, the need to be reminded is nothing new. Morality stories dominate the Old and New Testaments with the patriarch Abraham most commonly cited as the archetype of kindness for his hospitality to three Angels in human disguise. I initially thought to present his story for this blessing, but decided that the tiny tent above the Hebrew text would suffice as a meme for it.

As I continued my research, I came to prefer the concept of kindness exemplified in *Megillat Ruth* (Book Of Ruth). Found in the **Ketuvim** or Writings volume of the Torah, it seemed more compelling since there were no obvious supernatural elements at play. Upon being told to return to her people after the death of her young husband, Ruth, a Moabite woman insists on remaining with her widowed Israelite mother-in-law, Naomi. Her statement, *"Where you go I will go, and where you stay I will stay. Your people will be my people and your God my God,"* became the takeaway message that defined love, loyalty and sincere concern for another human being's welfare. It also painted Naomi as possibly the best mother-in-law in history! This story not only showcases our capacity for personal empathy, it also references the concept of 'gleaning', a mandated act of kindness towards an entire community of impoverished men, widows and orphans. Gleaning is the practice of allowing these individuals to reap the corners of one's fields and orchards for food following the initial harvest.

Representing those fields is a stone wall behind Ruth and Naomi. The sheaf of wheat and sprigs of barley, olives, figs and grapes are also memes for this idea, as is the pomegranate branch in Ruth's hand. I included the pomegranate for the connection of its seeds to the *613 mitzvot* (commandments) and its association with fertility. In the story, Ruth's actions will enable the continuation of Naomi's line, for she will become great-grandmother to King David.

Additionally, my illustration includes a small Hebrew letter *'chet'* (pronounced gutturally) formed by three sheaves of wheat that hover above and between the two women. It begins the words *'chittah'* (wheat) and *chesed* which means kindness and suggests the limitless loving-kindness that characterizes G-d and suffuses all of creation. The verse from **Pirke Avot** *1:2* (Ethics of the Fathers) attributed to the Second century High Priest Shimon HaTzaddik (Simon The Righteous) makes this clear: *"The world exists through three things: Torah, Avodah (Temple service) and acts of loving kindness."*

No matter how small or insignificant these deeds may seem when they occur, each one is ultimately a part of the larger purpose for which we were created.

THE BLESSING OF WISDOM:
From Night Into Day

The blessings in this book were not consciously created in any particular order. Nor do I subscribe to coincidence. Yet the familiar phenomenon of synchronicity always seemed to hover nearby knowing somehow just when to reveal itself. It must have been especially gleeful the day I began this blessing for the wisdom to distinguish between night and day. Sensing the transition from standard to daylight savings time is usually instinctive to most of us, but when it occurred at *2AM* that morning, I was totally taken by surprise and inconveniently overslept. Ignoring the fact that daylight savings time is entirely a human construct, the decision for which blessing to do next was a no-brainer.

The original title of this blessing, *'The Wisdom of the Rooster'* makes it unique among the many we have for expressing appreciation of our physical, mental and environmental gifts. Instead of thanking our Creator for our own ability to distinguish between night and day, we offer praise for *"giving the rooster understanding to distinguish between night and day."* Perhaps this idea is our reminder that because so much of our existence depends on the special abilities of many creatures great and small, it is incumbent on us to acknowledge our Creator through them.

In every day there are periods of light characterized by clarity, blessing, peace of mind and prosperity. As a balance there are also patches of darkness marked by challenge, confusion and difficulty. It takes maturity to look beyond the darkness and see the light that awaits us. In this way we learn from the rooster who symbolizes an attitude filled with optimism, hope and belief, teaching us to anticipate and celebrate blessing even before it appears.

These ideas are made manifest by a tiny rooster perched on the roof of the medieval-style house in my illustration. The central image is a sort of cosmic hourglass in which the sun and moon are suspended within their separate spheres. They are poised to reverse their positions in a dance designed at Creation. Our understanding of these celestial bodies as they relate to our lives and environment is represented by the couple praying near trees and houses, all juxtaposed with a man-made timekeeping device. The sprinkle of stars that inspired the signs of the Zodiac on the hourglass are there to remind us that while our acquired knowledge is of great value, the light of that value darkens without the wonder and faith that guide it.

BIRKAT KOHANIM:
A Blessing Of Connection For Peace & Protection

Fans of the Star Trek television series and its inscrutable Vulcan Mr. Spock like to reference their admiration by raising their hand in the strange configuration shown in my illustration. Since the actor, Leonard Nimoy is Jewish, it is only logical that he affected this gesture from an ancient Hebrew custom, the **Birkat Kohanim**, or Priestly Blessing. Its basis is the biblical verse: *"They shall place My name upon the children of Israel, and I Myself shall bless them"*, found in **BaMidbar** (Numbers) 6:23-27 where Aaron, the first Levitical High Priest and his sons bless the nascent Israelites. This oldest of known biblical texts was later adapted by individuals for personal use and has been found inscribed on amulets that date to the First Temple period beginning in *957 BCE*, some of which are currently in the collection of the Israel Museum in Jerusalem.

According to David Abudirham, a *13th* century Spanish Torah scholar, the **Birkat Kohanim** is unconventional because while it doesn't begin with *"Blessed Are You…"* it is still a prayer for peace and protection. Traditionally recited in a synagogue during the major festivals, it expresses the joy and good will of these celebrations. The *Birkat* differs from others in that only one or more *Kohanim* (descendants of Aaron and the priestly Tribe of Levi) may recite it. Subsequent interpretations extended its use to rabbis for blessing children at their bar or bat mitzvot and to parents who wish to bless their children before the Sabbath meal. On these occasions, it is usually introduced with a phrase requesting G-d to endow these children with the admirable qualities of Ephraim and Manasseh, the sons of Joseph or the Matriarchs Sarah, Rebecca, Rachel and Leah.

The **Birkat Kohanim** is replete with arcane symbols that invited visual interpretation. The hands, held spread out beneath a prayer shawl over the congregation with fingers and thumbs are positioned to create five apertures. These refer to the verses in the *Song of Songs* (2:8-9), which declare that while G-d remains hidden, He peers through the cracks in the 'wall', watching over and protecting Israel. In addition, the **Birkat** contains fifteen words corresponding to the fourteen joints of the fingers and to the palms of the hands to represent the fifteenth word of the blessing, *'shalom'* or peace. Accordingly, I've taken artistic license to mark the joints of the hands with letters of the Hebrew alephbet signifying the numbers *1 to 15*. Since this blessing originated during Jewish history's tribal era, I've included an interpretation of the *choshen* or breastplate worn by the high priest during Temple services. Its elaborate frame supports twelve precious stones, each representing one of the twelve tribes of Israel whose 'logos' frame the blessing. As I worked on the **Birkat Kohanim**, I recalled my own fondness for the Star Trek series and realized that Spock's ubiquitous salute introduced me to a facet of Judaism that would infuse my artwork with mystical speculation for the rest of my creative life.

And that turns out to be an inadvertent blessing, indeed.

MEZUZAH:
A Blessing Between Worlds

When we enter or leave a space through a doorway, most of us rarely wonder about the evanescent consequences of doing so. Yet, without considering that doorway as a bridge between worlds, we remain unaware of subtle changes in ourselves that occur through our experiences on either side of it. *Mezuzot*, those small boxes on the doorposts of traditional Jewish homes serve as memory tools for our awareness of these transitions and of the eternal unity of G-d as they guard the home's residents from harm. This tradition may have originated when the early Israelites marked their doorways for protection from the tenth plague (Death of the Firstborn) during the first Passover in Egypt over three thousand years ago.

Mezuzot, made in various sizes and materials, are often beautifully crafted works of art. They bear a single Hebrew letter *shin* or three Hebrew letters *shin, dalet, yud* that represent one of G-d's holy names. Inside is a *klaf* or tiny rolled parchment written by a *sofer* (scribe). Its two verses from the Torah; *Devarim* (Deuteronomy) *6:4-9* and *11:13-21* are written in 22 equally spaced lines. The *klaf* must be placed upright under the Hebrew letters in the box so the prayer will appear correctly. When we first occupy a new home, a blessing is recited just before installing a *mezuzah* on its doorpost taking care to secure it at the upper right-hand side, tilted toward the home's interior. This procedure is repeated for *mezuzot* installed at each doorway in the home except for the bathroom. Entering and leaving those spaces is then acknowledged with a touch to the *mezuzah* followed by a brief kiss to the hand that touched it, invoking G-d's blessing and protection on our comings and goings.

It is important to know that over time, the *klaf* may become damaged and should be periodically examined by a *sofer* who can repair any broken letters and preserve its effectiveness. The protective energies of the *mezuzah* have not always gone unchallenged in Jewish history. In Talmudic times, *mezuzot* were attributed with powers to ward off evil spirits, but by the Middle Ages, the Kabbalah's esoteric knowledge of various angels, magical phrases and mystical diagrams attained popularity and were added to the Torah verses. This latter practice lost momentum when the RamBam (an acronym for the 12th century French Rabbi and Talmudist Rabbeinu Mosheh Ben Maimon) asserted that writing Hebrew letters on the *mezuzah* case itself and for the prescribed verses within was acceptable, but those who wrote angelic names or other formulae on the inside would lose their share in *Olam Ha-Ba* (The World To Come).

Accordingly, the *mezuzah* in my illustration displays the Hebrew letter *shin* on the outside and only the Torah verses on the *klaf* within. The *22* verses from the interior *klaf* also appear in the background with some artistic license. The tiny gold pomegranate suspended from the *mezuzah* signifies abundance, fertility and the *613* categories of *mitzvot* (commandments). An equally tiny hand with its apotropaic eye crowns the *mezuzah*. This is called a *hamsa*, inspired by those ancient amulets employed to ward off evil throughout the Middle East.

On a personal note, though I've always had *mezuzot* in my home, it was only some years ago after a health crisis that I thought to have them checked for damage. Indeed, the *sofer* informed me, several critical letters had become damaged and the *klaf* needed to be repaired, a pronouncement that caused chills to run down my spine…

ברוך אתה ה' אלקינו מלך העולם, אשר קדשנו במצוותיו וצונו לקבוע מזוזה.

Blessed are You, Source Of Life, Who Sanctifies us With Your Mitzvot & Commands us to Affix a Mezuzah.

KADDISH:
A Blessing For Solace & Redemption

My decision to include the *Mourner's Kaddish* in this collection was a rather difficult one. Since I've always associated this blessing with death and mourning, I initially did not like the idea of incorporating a somber element in this book. It also seemed to be more of a prayer rather than a blessing. But before dismissing it entirely, I learned from my sources that the word *kaddish* translates as 'sanctification' and the prayer itself is for the sanctification of G-d's Name, meant to express praise and the profound desire for the perfection of all Creation. The *Kaddish* was never intended to be about the finality of death at all!

Instead of Hebrew, it was written in Aramaic as this was the common language spoken by Jews nearly 1400 years ago during the period of the destruction of the First Temple and through the completion of the Talmud. At that time, the prayer was considered important enough so that everyone could understand it.

My illustration for the *Mourner's Kaddish* includes two sources of light and remembrance shown in the lower left corner; an ancient clay oil lamp and a sturdy candle impaled on a medieval pewter candlestick. These reflect an allusion found in the Book of Proverbs *(20:27)* that considers the soul of man to be G-d's candle. In Judaism, candles are the universal symbol for the *nitzotz* or divine spark that enlivens our bodies. And in spiritual meditation, we are encouraged to allow a space in ourselves for G-d's Light to illuminate us for our own benefit and for our interactions with others.

Perhaps this idea can be understood as a reflection of the process of *'tzimtzum'* (contraction). The Kabbalah explains how G-d, during the process of Creation, made a space within His own being where our world and we might exist. Floating above the clay oil lamp is the Hebrew letter *zayin*. It corresponds to the number seven in *gematria* or Hebrew numerology. The *zayin* illustrates that the seven words beginning with the first *'Amen'* in the *Mourner's Kaddish* are comprised of twenty-eight letters. When the *'Amen'* ('so be it') is included, the verse contains eight words. This may seem like an obscure nit of information, but in esoteric Jewish philosophy, the number six represents our material world while the number seven represents the spirituality contained within that world. Since traditional belief maintains that our material world was created in six days, then the Sabbath or the seventh day became the spiritual catalyst that would complete it. The number eight represents that spiritual catalyst's ability to move beyond the world as we comprehend it.

Finally, the number twenty-eight is the numerical attribution of the Hebrew word *'koach'* or strength, which tells us that when we say the prayer with all of our strength, we can connect to the spiritual dimensions that allow us to virtually transcend our material world.

THE SEVENTH BLESSING:
For Love & Life

The Seven Blessings or **Sheva Brachot** are a lovely old tradition, each one recited under the *chuppah* (marriage canopy) by chosen friends and family at Jewish weddings. They begin with the *'pri hagofen'* (blessing over wine) followed by praise and gratitude to the Source of Life for our creation, for our existence and for our ability to thrive through time. They also address the binding of the couple, wishing them a life of love, joy, peace and friendship from the Biblical perspective; that their union should mirror the happiness of the first couple in the Garden of Eden. Finally, the new couple is made aware that as they rejoice in each other, their union will also bring joy to the world.

Initially, I attempted to work all seven blessings into my illustration. However, I soon learned that the seventh blessing is the most significant as it summarizes and encompasses the other six. This idea was suggested by a reading in Kabbalah that explains how each of the seven blessings corresponds to one of seven *sefirot* or the energies that are the foundation of Creation. Although there are actually ten *sefirot*, the interpretation posits that the three remaining *sefirot* do not correspond to their own blessings because two of them, *Keter* (crown representing ethereal consciousness) and *Chokhmah* (representing wisdom) are contained in the *sefirah* of *Binah* (understanding) and the last one, *Malkhut* receives all of those above and before it. The Hebrew language in the **Seventh Blessing** also contains ten words or synonyms for happiness, peace and friendship, all of which lead to joy. In this sense, it corresponds to all ten *sefirot* as well as the ten phrases by which the world was created and the Ten Commandments given at Mt. Sinai.

These ideas prompted me to place the letter *Bet (for Binah)* in the space above the *chuppah* for this value must guide all that we are and do. In addition to the *kallah* (bride) and *chossen* (groom) beneath the *chuppah* in their medieval splendor, my illustration incorporates a golden *kiddush* (wine) cup and a large ceremonial wedding ring to evoke those used in wedding ceremonies throughout Europe in the *15th-18th* centuries. Such costly elaborate rings were often the property of the Jewish community, loaned to the bridal couple for the ceremony to be replaced later by a standard gold wedding band. The tiny castle atop the ring symbolized their new home and Solomon's Temple recalling a pivotal period in Jewish history. The doves perched in the trees that support the chuppah represent the sacrifices the couple must make individually and together if their union is to be harmonious.

In the banners above and below the *chuppah* are traditional good wishes for the new couple. They read: *"L'Chaim"*(To Life) and *"Kol Shoshon v' kol Simcha, Kol Chattan v' Kol Kallah"* (All Joy and Gladness, Groom and Bride). Rabbi Aryeh Kaplan observes that from a greater spiritual perspective, Jewish weddings reflect the giving of the Torah at Mt. Sinai, an event that also symbolizes the wedding of Heaven and Earth and the zenith of human and divine joy.

BLESSING FOR THE SABBATH CANDLES:
Illuminating The Seventh Day

It is sundown on Friday night. As this woman rotates her hands in blessing above the two candles she has lit, you can imagine her singing *Shalom Aleichem* (Peace Unto You, O Ministering Angels), the traditional chant of peace that ushers in the Sabbath. This twenty-four hour period of rest from sundown to sunset is a central tenet of the Jewish faith. Both the song and her circular gestures are inspired by an early Talmudic legend of two ministering angels representing the divine dualities of good and evil. They are charged with escorting a Sabbath observer home from the synagogue on Friday night and determining whether the *Shekhinah* (Sabbath Queen and feminine aspect of the Divine) has been honored or dishonored by the level of observance. Accordingly, judgement on the family table is rendered.

The Sabbath mirrors the completion of Creation on the seventh day after it began and defines a space in our lives where we can cease our week's efforts and open our senses to those things that we rush past during the week. At its conclusion with the *havdalah* (separation) ceremony, we are refreshed as we resume our activities and begin the new week ahead. The *havdalah* blessings appear separately in this book.

On her lace tablecloth a *kiddush* cup filled with wine and two challahs that have been baked fresh for the Sabbath. The two challahs symbolize the double portion of *manna* given to the Israelites in the desert to honor the Sabbath. They are covered with an embroidered cloth that reads, *Shabbat Shalom* (Sabbath Peace). The candelabrum with its sheaf of golden wheat and pomegranates is designed to recall the altar from the ancient Temple where the Israelites brought the gifts of their harvest as offerings. The spirit figure in the background represents the *Shekhinah* whom we welcome into our homes for this brief time each week.

It is said that for the duration of the Sabbath, we are given an extra *neshomah* or soul that increases our understanding of Torah and enables us to experience union with our Creator. This gift also allows us a taste of the *Olam Ha Bah* or The World To Come. To merit even this brief enlightenment makes Sabbath observance even more compelling...

BLESSINGS FOR HAVDALAH:
A Ceremony Of The Senses

Although Judaism encompasses a complex set of holidays and rituals throughout the year, the Sabbath observance and the *Havdalah* ceremony that completes it are of primary importance. Tradition holds that Jews receive an extra soul or *neshomah* during the twenty-four hours of the Sabbath. According to the Chabad Hasidic philosophy, the spiritual architecture of the soul is a construct of five ascending levels of awareness and communion with G-d. *Neshomah* is only one but it is the highest level of awareness; the others are known as *Nefesh, Ruach, Chaya* and *Yechidah*. Each level has its own enigmatic character. The *Havdalah* ceremony re-awakens our senses from their respite to prepare us for the week ahead and is a formal way of bidding farewell to the *neshomah's* holy aspect until the following Sabbath arrives.

An essential part of the *Havdalah* service involves a *besamim* (spice container). I am always inspired by the beauty and functionality of these objects, many of which are crafted of precious metals and modeled after medieval castles and towers throughout Europe. Spice containers were often made this way to remind us that spices were once difficult to obtain and therefore very expensive. These treasured commodities were kept securely locked within castles or towers in each town and carefully rationed to each citizen. For its part in the ceremony, the *besamim* is filled with a mixture of fragrant spices such as cloves, cinnamon and nutmeg and passed in turn to each participant in the ceremony so they may experience the blessing of our sense of smell. Other aspects of the *Havdalah* ceremony include blessings recited over a *kiddush* cup (goblet of wine) and a specially braided large candle whose four wicks are simultaneously lit. This candle has multiple wicks to remind us of the duality of diversity and unity that characterizes the Jewish people. Each of these components remind us of the separation between the sacred and profane.

My illustration for this blessing visualizes the elements of the *Havdalah* service as presented by participants from the many lands where Jews have lived. The central figure balances a spice tower nestled in his *shtremel* (fur hat) as he carries the *Havdalah* candle and *kiddush* cup. Other *besamim* can be seen on the horizon where the sun has set. The other travelers bear plants and flowers that represent the various spices that may be used. All are gathered on a chequered isle designed as a metaphor of the space in time that is the Sabbath.

THE HA-MAPIL:
A Blessing To The Giver Of Sleep

Experiencing a restful night's sleep naturally with or without notable dreams and waking up refreshed is a gift, albeit it a rare one in this era of 24/7 media where one our most common complaints is the inability to fall asleep at the end of the day.

Indeed, this difficulty has become a problem of epidemic proportions, one that has made the pharmaceutical industry and medical 'sleep professionals' thrive. To their credit, medical 'sleep professionals' frequently advocate 'good sleep hygiene': putting aside all external stimuli before initiating sleep, yet they will still prescribe pharmaceutical sleep aids at a patient's request.

Setting science aside for the moment, Judaism offers us its own version of 'good sleep hygiene': by giving us the opportunity to recite the a set of prayers called the *Birkat Kriat Shema al Hamittah* (Evening Shema) at bedtime and obliging us to do so without the distraction of books or electronic media. If one is going to converse with the Source of Life, one had better be paying attention.

The three essential parts of the *Birkat Kriat Shema al Hamittah* are drawn from Torah verses found in: *Devarim* (Deuteronomy)*6: 5-9, 11:13-21* and *BaMidbar* (Numbers) *15: 37-41*. Additional readings from *Tehillim* (Psalms) may be added: *91, 3:2-9,* and *128*. The first is a prayer composed by Rabbi Isaac Luria, the 16th century Kabbalist that begins, *"Ribbono shel Olam"* (Master of the Universe). With it, one may request forgiveness for misdeeds done that day and state one's forgiveness of offense or injury done by others to him or her. Next is the *Ha-Mapil*, a personal meditation and a request for our souls to safely leave and return to our bodies at night and when we wake. Last is the *Shema* itself which addresses the Oneness of our Creator.

Of the three, the *Shema* and the *Ha-Mapil* are considered elemental. Both Ashkenazic and Sephardic Jews traditionally recite all three of them but opinions differ as to the order in which they should be recited. The *Mishnah Brurah* (a commentary on the first section of the *Shulchan Aruch* or Code of Jewish Law) says that natural instinct should be followed. If one cannot remain awake long enough to recite all three, then it is advised to recite only the *Ha-Mapil*.

For this illustration, I have presented the *Birkat Ha-Mapil* and two parts of the *Shema* after the Sephardic *minhag* (custom). These float through the night sky as a woman recites them, covering her eyes with her hand to focus her concentration. They are punctuated only by a fanciful allegorical figure: a heavenly messenger transporting her soul to G-d for safekeeping until morning. A variant of this figure also appears departing from the woman in the morning *Modeh Ani* blessing. The night-blooming datura or Trumpet Flower whose essences are legendary in Indian and Chinese cultures for their pain-relieving properties, is an analogy for sleep because it temporarily relieves any pain we've experienced that day, a true gift from the Giver Of Sleep.

הודו ליהוה כי־טוב כי לעולם חסדו.
O Give Thanks To The Lord For He Is Good
For His Mercy Endureth ForEver.

לעשה השמים בתבונה...
To Him That By Understanding Made The Heavens,

לרקע הארץ על־המים...
To Him That Spread Forth The Earth Above The Waters,

לעשה אורים גדלים...
To Him That Made The Great Lights,

את־השמש לממשלת ביום...
The Sun To Rule By Day.

את־הירח וכוכבים לממשלות בלילה.
The Moon & Stars To Rule By Night.

נתן לחם לכל בשר
Who Giveth Food To All Flesh,

הודו לאל השמים כי לעולם חסדו.
פסוק קלו...
O Give Thanks To The Lord Of Heaven,
For His Mercy Endureth ForEver.
••• Psalm 136

The text of this book was set in **_Centaur,_** a humanist type family commissioned by the Metropolitan Museum of Art and drawn in *1914* by Bruce Rogers. The typeface design was based on the work of several Renaissance era typographers: Nicholas Jenson *(1469)* for his *Eusebius* font: the forerunner of the modern Roman alphabet, Francesco Griffo *(1495)* for a book by Pietro Bembo titled *De Aetna* and Ludovico Arrighi *(1520)* from his chancery face, which simulated fifteenth century handwriting and influenced the *italic* form of the Centaur font.

About The Author

Ilene Winn-Lederer, a native of Chicago, attended The Art Institute of Chicago and The Chicago Academy of Fine Arts. She currently resides in the US in Pittsburgh, Pennsylvania, writing books and creating original imagery that navigate the delicate bridge between the mundane and mystical theaters of human experience. These are published under her imprint, *Imaginarius Editions.* Other titles listed at the front of this book may be seen at: *www.winnlederer.com.*

Ilene is also the author and illustrator of **Between Heaven & Earth: An Illuminated Torah Commentary** *(Pomegranate, 2009).* A board member of the *Pittsburgh Society of Illustrators,* Winn-Lederer's clients have included *The New York Times, The Wall Street Journal, Hadassah, NY., Lilith Magazine, Children's Television Workshop, Scholastic, Charlesbridge Publishers, Simon & Schuster and Cricket Magazine.*

Her unique drawings and paintings are included in public and private collections throughout the United States and Europe.
The Magic Eye Gallery at *www.magiceyegallery.com* offers original works and custom gicleé prints with a wink from her mind's eye…